I0481837

Make Money Online: 7 Proven Methods for Making Your Very First $1 on The Internet in 2018 and Beyond

By Oliver El-Gorr

You recognize and agree that we have made no implications, warranties, promises, suggestions, projections, representations or guarantees whatsoever to you about future prospects or earnings, or that you will earn any money, with respect to your purchase of books by Oliver El-Gorr, and that we have not authorized any such projection, promise, or representation by others.

Any earnings or income statements, or any earnings or income examples, are only estimates of what we think you could earn. There is no assurance you will do as well as stated in any examples. If you rely upon any figures provided, you must accept the entire risk of not doing as well as the information provided. This applies whether the earnings or income examples are monetary in nature or pertain to advertising credits which may be earned (whether such credits are convertible to cash or not).

There is no assurance that any prior successes or past results as to earnings or income (whether monetary or advertising credits, whether convertible to cash or not) will apply, nor can any prior successes be used, as an indication of your future success or results from any of the information, content, or strategies. Any and all claims or representations as to income or earnings (whether monetary or advertising credits, whether convertible to cash or not) are not to be considered as "average earnings".

The Economy. The economy, both where you do business, and on a national and even worldwide scale, creates additional uncertainty and economic risk. An economic recession or depression might negatively affect the results produced by Oliver El-Gorr.

Your Success Or Lack Of It. Your success in using the information or strategies provided by Oliver El-Gorr depends on a variety of factors. We have no way of knowing how well you will do, as we do not know you, your background, your work ethic, your dedication, your motivation, your desire, or your business skills or practices. Therefore, we do not guarantee or imply that you will get rich, that you will do as well, or that you will have any earnings (whether monetary or advertising credits, whether convertible to cash or not), at all.

Internet businesses and earnings derived therefrom involve unknown risks and are not suitable for everyone. You may not rely on any information presented on the website or otherwise provided by us, unless you do so with the knowledge and understanding that you can experience significant losses (including, but not limited to, the loss of any monies paid to purchase books by Oliver El-Gorr, and/or any monies spent setting up, operating, and/or marketing books by Oliver El-Gorr, and further, that you may have no earnings at all (whether monetary or advertising credits, whether convertible to cash or not).

Contents

Make Money Online: 7 Proven Methods for to Make Your Very First $1 on The Internet in 2018 and Beyond

Free Bonus

As a thank you for downloading this book, I have a special bonus for you. It focuses on the second part of the online entrepreneurship equation, namely - your mindset

Many people don't start out with the correct mindset to be a successful online entrepreneur, I know I didn't.

So I wrote this guide as a way to help you undo some of the bad programming you may have acquired throughout your life, through no fault of your own.

There are also a number of habits that all successful entrepreneurs have, and I've noted those down as well.

Your free copy includes:

- The most important question to ask yourself before you begin your online business
- The one thing you can count on in business and in life
- One big mindset tip most business books won't tell you
- Why being arrested for insider trading was actually a good thing for this one businessman
- How to effectively set both business and personal goals
- Why saying morning affirmations *won't* make your rich

You can get your copy for free by going to this link

http://el-gorr.com/unbreakable

Introduction

Or for a more appropriate title...the who the hell am I and why am I writing this book section.

It wasn't until my sister told me "you know, being an entrepreneur is cool now" that I realized I was doing something with my life which people envied.

It makes sense in hindsight, we were in Thailand, chilling by the swimming pool of a lush jungle retreat in the North of the country. And I had already made more money by 9AM than I'd spend in the next week.

I now realize the beneficial consequence of the decisions I'd make up until that point.

It wasn't always like this though.

Cue the rags to riches tale. Or my version of it at least.

I had a fairly uneventful childhood. Raised in a middle class family, in a middle class town. Not much to report here. I graduated University in 2012, with a piece of paper which I believe is more commonly referred to as a "Bachelors degree", along with a healthy amount of student loan debt. This was as the world had just about fully recovered from the 2008 downturn - or so the news reports on TV told me.

What they didn't tell me was that in the UK at least - the job situation for young people like myself was getting worse. Graduate salaries had stagnated over the past 15 years, while the cost of living had risen significantly. This was magnified by me living in London at the time, where house prices continued to soar despite the recent recession.

I was faced with a decision, move back in with my parents for the foreseeable future, or spend 50% of my monthly paycheck to rent a windowless room in a house which was still at least an hour commute away from my newly acquired job.

I chose the former - it was a terrible move.

While I saved some money, I still commuted for nearly 3 hours every day to a job I intensely disliked - all to acquire enough money to have the ability to do the same thing the next month.

Talk about a treadmill lifestyle.

They say to get a glimpse into your future, you should look at the people who have been at your job for 15-20 years.

One look around me confirmed for me that I did not want to continue along this career path.

And then I discovered this one simple trick which gave me money on autopilot!

No, I'm kidding, there was no magic button solution, nor will there ever be one. In my case at least, it was just a lot of experiments with various online income streams until something finally stuck.

Fast forward 4 years, and I am now in a good place with my online income. I have multiple businesses which generate me enough money each month, which allow me to live wherever I want.

It's given me the freedom to visit 37 countries and live on 3 different continents. An opportunity which wouldn't have been possible otherwise.

There wasn't just a single business that allowed me to a achieve this, more a combination of them.

And later on in this book, I'll talk more about my favorite way of making money online for beginners in 2018. One which doesn't require any special skill to get started, nor does it require a huge amount of cash up front.

I'm going to make any huge promises, I'm not going to tell you that you'll become a millionaire overnight. The only thing I'm promising you here is that if you follow the advice given inside this book, you will make your very first $1 online.

Yep, that's it - $1. There's no make-$100,000-a-day-with-just-15 minutes-work type stuff here.

It's not much, but it's a start. More importantly, it's a start that will give you the momentum and confidence to keep going in your online business journey.

Oh - one more thing, I'm not going to pitch you a get rich quick scheme, Multi-Level Marketing (MLM) or network marketing "opportunity" if that's what you're thinking. What I have to offer over the next few chapters is far more legitimate and useful to your online career.

But before we get into it, let's discuss some problem people have with making money online, and what you can do to avoid them.

Thanks,

Oliver

Why do so many people fail online?

Before we begin talking about the various ways you can make money using the internet, we should address the elephant in the room. Why do so many online entrepreneurs fail?

This question doesn't have a simple answer, and any answer I can give you will be multi-faceted. It's both a question of mechanics, in other words, the business model you are using, and also a question of mindset, and whether or not you have the right one.

Let's talk about mechanics first, many online business ventures have certain hurdles you must overcome to go from simply "doing" them, to making money with them. What I mean by this is, anyone can start writing a blog and make zero money with it. However, very few people learn how to monetize their blog and make a living from it. The same goes with a YouTube channel, for instance, you can have a channel which gets a lot of views in each video, but if you don't have a monetization strategy - then you might as well be dead in the water.

Other businesses have certain financial hurdles like needing an upfront investment or needing particular technical skills in order to execute them successfully. Skills like how to acquire traffic (people clicking on your site/store), copywriting (how to sell with words) or web development. Fortunately, these are skills which can be learned over time, and ones you should consider learning when building your online business. Don't worry if you don't have a lot of money or any particular skills though, I'll be discussing those more later on in this book.

Which brings me to my second point - your mindset. The reason so many people fail online is simply a matter of quitting. They run into their first struggle as an online entrepreneur and decide it would just be easier to go back to their 9 to 5 job.

Let me say this now, it is not going to be a matter of snapping your fingers and making money online in 2018, if I told you otherwise then I would be lying to you. There is a learning curve to this, and you will have setbacks along the way. The big difference between a 9 to 5 job and an online business is self reliance. With the latter, you are your own boss, and thus the responsibility lays with you. So it's up to you, and you only, which determines whether you will succeed.

However, if you have a built-in resiliency, and determination to succeed at this, then you will. You will uncover the right parts to success. You will acquire the right skills. You will set up successful business ventures, that is certain. For some people, the path will be shorter, and less obstacle-filled. For others, it may take some more time, but one thing is certain, if you truly, deep down, want to make this work for you - then you will.

That isn't all there is to the mindset part of the game, but I'll be discussing that more in-depth later on in the book.

The three core online business models

In the very simplest of terms, there are 3 main online business models. Pretty much every method of making money online can be divided into one of these three categories.

The first of which is the service-based business model, where you provide a service for an individual or a company in exchange for financial compensation. This can be anything from freelancing, to coaching or consulting.

The second is ecommerce, or selling your own products online. This is one of the oldest and time tested methods of making money on the internet. Nowadays we can't imagine a world without giants like Amazon and eBay, but it's entirely possible to get started on a smaller scale with your own ecommerce business. You probably won't be getting Jeff Bezos level income overnight, but it's entirely possible to make a decent living in your spare time with an ecommerce business.

Now when it comes to ecommerce there a few different options there, but before we discuss them we should probably break them down into two categories.

Selling physical products - Ones you can hold in your hand, anything from essential oils to slime containers to silicone kitchen utensils to imported chandeliers. Whatever it is, you can sell it online.

Selling information products - These are digitally delivered products like ebooks, video courses and audio recordings. These products usually center around teaching people a certain skill.

The third way of making money online is affiliate marketing. Where you promote other people's products in exchange for a commission on every sale that you make.

However, before we discuss each of these and the various options available in more detail, I'd like to tell you about a quick marketing lesson which they don't teach you in school.

Learning this alone will give you a huge leg up on your competition in whichever online business venture you decide to go into.

The most important marketing lesson you will ever learn

How's that for a big claim? Well, it's one which everyone should learn at the outset of their internet entrepreneurial journey. Many people don't learn this after years and years of trying and failing. But the ones that learn it early on are often the most successful.

The lesson is this

No one cares about you - they only care about themselves

Now what does that statement mean? It means, any business you approach, you must do so from the point of view of your customer or client.

If you have an idea for a product, ask yourself this before sinking money into it - does anyone really want this? Has anyone ever expressed a desire for this? Are people already buying products similar to this?

You may think your combination toaster oven and beer cooler is a fantastic invention, but you must gauge the demand for it before you spend thousands getting that expensive prototype made.

It's the same if you are running a service based business. Do you find yourself trying to sell clients on your services just by using what are called "I statements". Things like "I have 10 years of experience", "I'm a great graphic designer". As a client, no one really cares about your credentials, they only care about what you can do for them. Do credentials matter? Somewhat. However, most people would rather hire someone who is enthusiastic and reliable, and most importantly - truly understands their needs, over the most qualified person in the world who doesn't.

Back in my freelancing career, I would routinely win jobs over more qualified candidates because I could demonstrate to the client that I understood their needs, and wasn't focused on my own.

Now, if you can approach all your business ventures from this point of view, you will almost instantly be better positioned than 80% of your competition.

Running a service based business

We'll cover this one first because it's one of the few businesses mentioned on here where you can get started for absolutely zero money. I'm assuming you already own a laptop or desktop computer and have an internet connection - so your core "necessities" for making this kind of business work, are completely covered.

In terms of types of service based businesses, I'll break it down into freelancing and then coaching/consulting work. This type of business model are near identical, but in most cases, it is necessary to go through one before you get to the other.

Freelancing

Freelancing is great because unlike dropshipping, affiliate marketing or any other online work, you can make money from day 1 without spending a single penny on inventory or months building up an email list. It's also how I got my start making money online.

Every day there are millions of potential clients on the internet looking for someone to do a job for them. This can be something as simple as writing a blog post, to more complex jobs like designing a website or even building a piece of software based on the client's vision.

Where do you find these clients you say?

Upwork

Upwork is currently the biggest online freelancing marketplace in the world. Every day over 10,000 jobs are posted on the site. Those jobs collectively pay millions to those who win the contracts. If you need to get some money together fast - Upwork is where you should go.

It gets a bad reputation in the freelancing world as many freelancers complain about low rates of pay and poor quality clients. A lot of that comes down to the freelancer themselves though, and how they conduct their freelancer business.

With over 12 million freelancers signed up, competition is fierce. However, the vast majority of freelancers don't know what they're doing and that's why I'm going to show you the competitive edges you need to win these jobs, increase your hourly rates and make a full-time living online by freelancing on Upwork.

The importance of niching down

This doesn't just apply to Upwork, but pretty much all internet based business models. It's better to be a big fish in a small pond than the other way around. Having a niche is vital because it's much easier to make money as a specialist in a world of generalists.

So instead of being a "writer", be a "food blog writer" or instead of being a generic "web designer", be a web designer who specializes in Squarespace based websites. This will instantly elevate you above generic candidates when clients are looking for freelancers for their jobs.

Another benefit of having a niche is that you only need a few good clients to provide you with enough work. Take it from experience when I say it is infinitely easier to work on 2 or 3 projects at once than it is to work on 6 or 7.

Common freelancing myth - believing you don't have any skills

Yes, you do, you just don't realize it yet.

Thanks to the internet, the vast majority of freelancing skills can be learned.

You don't need a computer science degree to charge $5,000+ for a website.

You don't need a copywriting degree (do these even exist?) to charge $150/hour.

You don't need to have graduated in video production or have 10 years industry experience to make a full time living freelancing in that area.

My very first job on Upwork was writing a product review for cat food. Yes, cat food. I'd never written a product review in my life. But guess what, I typed into Google "how to write a product review" and bam, I had the instructions in front of me. I got paid $3 for that job, not life changing income I know, but all that $3 did was give me the confidence of knowing that I could make money using the internet. That momentum creates a powerful snowball effect.

How to write a good Upwork profile

Your profile is your gateway to job invites. It's your chance to sell yourself and stand out in a sea of average freelancers. It's also how you are going to be found in Upwork's search engine and how you get recommended for public jobs that people post.

A lot of Upwork freelancers make a big mistake in their profile though - they look at it like a resume.

All they do talk about themselves and how great they are at their particular job. This sounds logical right?

Wrong. Dead wrong.

Clients don't care about your Master's degree (or lack of one), or your 7 years of corporate experience. All they care about is what you can do for them.

So let's flip the problem around. Who is your ideal client? What does your client want from you? What do you provide that other freelancers don't? You need to look at your profile from your client's point of view.

Here's a quick tip you can use regardless of your niche. Instead of having an "I" focused profile, which talks about yourself. Have a "you" focused profile which talks about your ideal client.

Another thing you can do when you have a bit of experience is focus on the results you get for your clients. Upwork clients can leave feedback after a job which appears on your public profile. You can use these as testimonials for future clients to see.

Quick 5-step Upwork profile checklist

1. Does your first sentence encourage a client to keep reading?
2. Do you address your potential client's needs/wants/desires?
3. Do you show that your previous work has achieved results?
4. Have you included keywords that clients are likely to search for?
5. Have you included a call-to-action at the end to get the client to take the next step?

Do this, and you'll have a better profile than 97% of Upwork freelancers. You'll be winning jobs in no time. In fact, some Upwork freelancers have used this method to make more than $3,000 in their very first month on the platform.

Now that's out the way, we'll cover the second part of the Upwork game, how to bid on public jobs

4 quick proposal tips you can use to win public jobs

1. Don't use a stock cover letter

Instead, customize each proposal to the needs of the client. Doing this alone will elevate you above most of your competition

2. Research your client

If they have a website, spend 5 minutes on it and get a feel for what they are looking for

3. Use a relevant work sample

If you don't have samples, make one up on the spot. If someone is looking for a freelancer to write blog posts about the best Mexican food in NYC, write a few hundred words about the best sushi in Houston. This way your sample is relevant without just giving the client free work. Never do free work on Upwork.

4.   Use a call to action

Every piece of communication you send should have a call to action (CTA). This can be as simple as asking a question about the job or inquiring if the client can discuss the project over Skype for 10 minutes. Nothing major, just give them one focused decision to make.

Send them very closed questions with only 1 possible answer. This way you can continue the conversation and then lead them down the path to closing a sale.

That just about covers Upwork for now. So let's graduate from there and discuss the higher level in coaching/consulting work.

Coaching/Consulting

If you already have an existing offline consulting or coaching based business, then you can conceivably skip the Upwork step and go out on your own straight away. I'd recommend doing this only if you have the ability to bring some of your existing clients with you.

The next step in running a service based business is moving from freelancing platforms like Upwork, into running your own business and having clients pay you directly rather than relying on platforms like Upwork as the middle man. You can make good money on Upwork, upwards of 6 figures a year if you're good, but if you want to take your income to the next level, then you need to move off the platform.

Here are a few reasons why

Get paid based on the value you provide to a person or business rather than for the time you spend with them

The biggest drawback of Upwork as a platform (and all other freelancing platforms for that matter) is that each freelancer has an hourly rate displayed by their name. This rate has a negative effect on a client's mind because they believe they are paying for your time rather than the value you provide. If they see your time as $500 per hour, the vast majority of clients will be reluctant to pay that. This is even if you can spend 1 day with them and put a plan into action where they will make an extra $50,000 over the course of the next 6 months.

However, if you operate independently, you can position yourself as a "pay for the value I provide for your business" type consultant versus a "pay for my hours" consultant. The former has the potential to net you far more money.

So how do you transition from being paid hourly, to being paid on value? Well there are a few ways you can go about it.

Sell to buyers

This sounds obvious but many freelancers, coaches and consultants get this wrong. They go around from business to business trying to convince them that they need a copywriter/graphic designer, when instead they should be looking at businesses who are already hiring for the same position. These businesses already understand the value that you provide, and thus are more likely to pay you what you are worth.

Be the expert

It's never been easier to position yourself as an expert than it is in 2018. There are so many sub-sub-sub niches for each industry that pretty much anyone can become the go-to guy or gal in their field. Remember, it's better to be a specialist than it is to be a generalist. If you're looking for titles or credentials, get yourself booked on podcasts or write and self publish a   book. This alone will separate you from the masses.

Arm yourself with testimonials

You can never have enough testimonials, one famous marketer has 47 pages of them on his website alone. That adds up to hundreds of people who will personally vouch for their services. Try to get testimonials from every client you work with (provided you do a good job). If you think that people won't want to give you one, it doesn't hurt to ask. They will very rarely say no.

Build an email list

There is no better way to connect with people and demonstrating (rather than just telling) your knowledge than having an email list. You can show people in your emails that you understand their problems, and in turn, that you have the solution to them.

An email list is vital because it's an asset that you own. You aren't relying on a third party platform or website, like you are with say YouTube, these are your customers and your audience. You can't be shut down by anyone and no one can take these people away from you.

Affiliate Marketing

Affiliate marketing is a common method of making money online. This is when you promote other people's products, and you get a percentage commission for every sale they make. Many businesses now rely solely on affiliates to get traffic and sales for their products, and it makes sense for both parties.

For a business owner or product creator, they have the luxury of not spending time or money on advertising, because their affiliates are taking care of all of that. Therefore they can spend their time making the product as quality as possible.

For the affiliate, they only have to drive traffic to the product itself. They don't have to worry about fulfilment or technical issues, because the product creator handles that. So if you already have an audience online, you can promote multiple products to them and get commissions.

The beauty of affiliate marketing as a business model is that you can use multiple sources of traffic to get people to the offer. For example, if you have a blog and a YouTube channel, you can do a written review of a certain product, and then a video review. Therefore you are capturing a large audience and your overall sales numbers will be higher.

Choose a quality product to promote

As an affiliate, your biggest challenge is promoting quality products. By this I mean ones with a low return rate. Unfortunately not all products are created equal, some are just cash grabs from the owner, and thus are largely useless. These products will have a high rate of return and thus you won't get any commissions.

Choose a product your audience needs

For example, if you're in the fitness niche then don't start promoting $1,000 computer software - because it's unlikely that your core audience has a use for this. So this will only alienate you from them. Instead consider promoting supplements or workout equipment.

Choose a product which will make you money

Depending on the affiliate program you use, commissions range between 3% and 90%. So if you're promoting a $100 product at 3% commissions, then you're only getting $3 for a sale. Whereas if you promote a $50 product with 50% commissions then you're getting $25 for a sale.

Ideally, you want products that either have a high initial value, or ones in which you get recurring commissions every month.

The first one is obvious, the higher the initial commissions, the better for you. Because you are spending the same amount of time promoting a product, but netting more money at the end of the day. So there's no point going all out if your commission is only a few dollars. But if you can find a quality product which nets you $100 commissions, then it is a more attractive option.

For recurring commissions, if you are promoting a subscription service in which the user pays $49 a month, and you are getting 50% recurring commissions, then you get $25 per month for every month they use that service. Which means you get a nice monthly check on autopilot, but only have to promote the product once.

Affiliate Networks

Amazon - Did you know Amazon has their own affiliate network? It's true, you can sign up and promote any Amazon product and receive a small commission in the process. As the commissions are low (3%), I would only recommend doing this passively - like on a "products I use" page on a blog for example. But it's a good chance to get started with affiliate marketing because customers trust Amazon so you don't need to do any convincing if the product is any good or not.

Clickbank - One of the largest affiliate networks in the world. Clickbank sells everything from making money online products to health supplements to workout plans. Clickbank often has higher commissions (40-60%), however, a large number of products on the site are poor quality - which can pose a problem because of high refund rates

JVZoo - Similar to Clickbank but with less products. I would say the quality of the products is about the same. There are some high ticket products ($1000 commissions) on here though which is why I decided to mention it

Individual Companies - If there's a product or service that you love, then see if they have an affiliate program. Many companies do so if you just type into Google "Company Name + Affiliate" you will see if there's one or not.

How to make money as an affiliate marketer

Making money as an affiliate marketer comes down to one key factor - your audience. Both the size of your audience and how much they trust you is important here. You aren't going to make a killing if your blog only gets 15 unique hits a week, or your average YouTube video gets 43 views.

Trust is the second factor, if you engage with your audience on a regular basis and stay consistent with a message which resonates with them, they are likely to trust product recommendations that you have.

Should you only recommend products that you have personally used?

This is a common question in the affiliate marketing space, and for me, the answer is no. Just because you haven't personally used a product, doesn't necessarily mean your audience won't find value from it. The key is to identify products which will benefit your audience and then promote those products. Remember, your audience is king here, so the best products to promote are ones which will help them rather than the ones which will merely bring you the highest commissions.

Where it does get questionable is if you use a direct competitor product, but then recommend a different one to your audience because the other product has a more generous affiliate program. I see this a lot with website hosting services, many bloggers recommend using Bluehost because they have a great affiliate program, but the blogger themselves uses Hostgator for their own site.

The Real Way to Make Money Blogging

This sounds great right, having a blog which you can share your personal thoughts and interests, and then make money from. However, it's not quite that easy. I don't want to be negative at any point during this book - because there's enough of that in the online and offline world. But I would be doing you a disservice if I told you that it's easy to make money with a "passion focused" blog. By passion focused I mean a blog that is personal to you, and then you promote affiliate products from. Only a tiny percentage of people make a full time living from these (despite what some might tell you).

The most popular "passion blog" categories

- Travel
- Food
- Parenting/Mom blogs
- Sewing (surprisingly enough)
- Health

- Fitness/Weight Loss
- Spirituality (notably Christian blogs)

As many of these blogs rely on sheer volume of traffic, their commission per sale is generally low. As mentioned in the previous chapter, a lot of these rely on Amazon affiliate sales only, which at 3% per sale - means you need to build up a huge audience.

At this point you're probably thinking that blogging is not for you - however, there is another way to make decent money with a blog that you may not have thought of

Enter...The SEO Optimized Product Review Blog

Have you ever searched for reviews for certain products, like say vacuum cleaners? You're likely going to find large authority sites like consumerreport.com and trustedreviews.com on the top of page 1.

But what if you decided to get more specific with your search and typed in "best vacuum cleaners for pet hair", now the first couple of sites which come up are as follows.

Rover.com

Spotlessvacuum.co.uk

Groomandstyle.com

Dogsrecommend.com

And the URL (exact web address) for all these sites is directly targeted to the phrase I have searched. So we'll take the 3rd example, the site URL which appears in the Google search is

Groomandstyle.com/best-vacuum-for-pet-hair/

This page has reviews of 8 different vacuum cleaners, with an affiliate link to each one included. So if I buy a vacuum cleaner through one of these links, then the site gets the commission. Now a single sale of a vacuum isn't going to make a lot of cash, after all, 3% of $249.99 is only $7.50 - but the search term "best vacuum cleaners for pet hair" has over 36,000,000 results in Google - which means a good amount of people are searching for it. This website being the 3rd result in Google means they are getting a lot of hits, and thus a lot of clicks on their affiliate links. It's not unreasonable to think the blog owner is making a full time living from this blog.

This is a far easier way of making money blogging than the original, "passion blog" example I gave. By targeting phrases shoppers are using and designing your website around them so they rank high in Google, you are likely to appear in front of a bigger audience than if you just have a regular old cooking blog.

So now it all comes down to identifying affiliate niches. The key is to become a big fish in a small pond. So don't try to hit a home run and become the #1 blog in the dog niche for example. Instead, why not try to become the go-to blog for owners of a certain breed like Huskies.

Then check out what affiliate programs are available for this niche. Like if you're in the dog niche, you can look at petsitting programs, products for dogs on Amazon etc. etc.

When you first start your blog, then the best thing to do is post extremely frequently. I'm talking bare minimum 3 times a day, and preferably every single day. Do this and you have a better chance of ranking well in Google. It's a lot of work up front, but once you get there, it's a lot easier to maintain - especially if you get one article in particular which gets a lot of views.

The best articles are in-depth review posts where you review a set amount of product, like the vacuum cleaner example I gave above. That particular post is over 4,400 words long and thus Google considers it "high quality content" which ranks well. I didn't count the number of affiliate links on the site but it's over 10 at least. So you can bet whoever owns this site is making a decent amount of money.

Remember, the key with these affiliate blogs is being optimized in line with what people are searching Google. So make sure you Search Engine Optimization (SEO) is on point. There are certain website plugins that can do this for you, Yoast is a popular one for Wordpress based blogs. Alternatively, you can hire a professional, but that won't be cheap. Fortunately, there are a number of decent free resources to help you get started with SEO, I recommend Neil Patel's blog neilpatel.com as a solid starting point.

But what if you're not much of a writer, maybe you're more of a talker? This leads me seamlessly to my next chapter.

The Real Way to Make Money with YouTube

Unless you've been living under a rock, you'll be familiar with YouTube - the largest video site on the internet. Here's a startling fact for you - more hours of video are uploaded to YouTube in a month than the 3 biggest US TV networks have produced since their inception over 60 years ago. YouTube is a more personal medium when compared with say a blog because you can actually see the person's face and hear their voice as opposed to just reading their words on a screen. Which makes it a fantastic platform for affiliate marketers and product creators.

Note, that I said these 2, and not just "making money from people watching your videos". Yes, YouTube has ads which you can enable on your videos if you have more than 1,000 subscribers - but these ads pay you, the creator, very little. The actual figure is somewhere around $0.5-$3 per 1000 views depending on the niche, and most niches are toward the lower end of that. It's also incredibly easy for YouTube to demonetize your channel for no apparent reason, which means you can't run ads on any of your videos.

Enough of the negative stuff, now let's get onto the positive. You can leverage YouTube to promote affiliate products or your own products.

For example, if you have an online course - you can use YouTube to build your audience and then send them to your course.

Alternatively, you can do product reviews for affiliate products you have used and then use your affiliate link in the YouTube description. Most large channels on YouTube make far more money from this affiliate method than they do from ad revenue based on just views.

The little known YouTube secret which doesn't involve showing your face

A big hang-up people have with YouTube is that they might not want to show their face, or be the center of attention. After all, it's a bit overwhelming at first to get on camera like that. However, there is another way to make money with YouTube that is really mentioned in making money online. And that is the "faceless" affiliate channel. This is when you simply have a channel of you reviewing products (usually information products like online courses), all you have to do is record a screencap of this with yourself talking. No need to show your face at all.

At this point you're probably thinking - how do I get my videos ranked in YouTube. There are two main methods, the keyword method, and the captivating title method.

The first one is pretty obvious, and similar to what you would do with a blog. You want to have your video title as the same phrase people are typing in for example

Self Publishing Blueprint Review - Is it the best Kindle publishing course for 2018?

People are already searching for the term "Self Publishing Blueprint Review" - so it's likely that your video will rank well.

The second method is using a captivating title. Now some people call this "clickbait", but for me, it only becomes clickbait when the video content doesn't live up to the title itself.

So an example for the same video content would be

Make up to $10,000 a month online with this self publishing course

That title naturally gets people curious, and you can talk about how some students of that particular course have made $10,000 a month in your video review. That way you pay off the claims you made in the title.

Some people go even further and they actually pay actors to portray themselves in the video, and they just write the review "script" for the actor to read on camera. Personally, I'm not a huge fan of this method as it is a bit disingenuous - but if the product review itself is real then it's still on the ethical side of things in my opinion.

Doing this allows you to tap into the social proof of having a person on camera which viewers can make themselves familiar with, but still allows you to have the ability to make money without showing your face.

Ecommerce

Ecommerce, or selling products online is one of the oldest methods of making money on the internet. Nowadays we can't imagine a world without giants like Amazon and eBay, but it's entirely possible to get started on a smaller scale with your own ecommerce business. You probably won't be getting Jeff Bezos level income overnight, but it's entirely possible to make a decent living in your spare time with ecommerce.

In fact, ecommerce as a whole is growing at an astounding rate. More than half (53%) of the internet users on the planet have now purchased something online. Global ecommerce sales are now projected to reach $4.5 trillion, yes trillion with a T, by the end of 2021.

Now there a few options here, but before we discuss them we should probably break them down into two categories.

Selling physical products - Ones you can hold in your hand, anything from essential oils to slime containers to silicone kitchen utensils to imported chandeliers. Whatever it is, you can sell it online.

Selling information products - These are digitally delivered products like ebooks, video courses and audio recordings. These products usually center around teaching people a certain skill.

Amazon FBA

What if there was a way where you could sell products, but have Amazon do all the shipping and handling for you? Well - that's where FBA or Fulfillment by Amazon comes in.

If you're completely new to this, FBA is when third party sellers sell white label (or private label) products via Amazon's website. Anyone can sign up for an account and do this. You simply send the items to one of Amazon's warehouses and upload your product description to the site.

So what kind of items can you sell, well the answer is nearly anything. The majority of categories on Amazon's website are unrestricted, meaning anyone can sell in them without needing to pass any checks beforehand. So as long as you don't infringe on anyone's trademark or patents, you're good to go.

To narrow it down a bit more, there are a number of metrics that FBA sellers use to determine the profitability of a product. I won't go into them in the book because it's not designed to be a guide to Amazon FBA, but if you are interested there are a few YouTube channels where you can learn the basics. One I recommend is Jungle Scout - they're an honest bunch, which is more than I can say for some of the larger presences in the Amazon FBA scene.

The beauty of Amazon FBA is that you don't have to build your own customer base (either organically or through paid advertising) like you would with a dropshipping store for example. You rely on Amazon's existing traffic, in other words, the volume of customers who are already searching for similar products for what you intend to sell.

Now I can hear you already saying - where on Earth do I get these products made?

China.

You get them made in China.

Shocking right? China has the biggest number of wholesalers out there and they will mass produce nearly anything you can think of. So FBA sellers find a product they want to sell on Amazon, have a manufacturer in China make any necessary modifications, put the seller's logo on the product, then ship it to one of Amazon's warehouses in the United States. Fascinating right? Isn't ecommerce great.

Most successful FBA sellers focus on products that do not have moving parts, do not go in or on your body. In other words, products with the least potential to "go wrong". These products usually have a price point which is firmly in the "impulse buy" range - so between $20-$50. You must be aware that Amazon takes around 30% of all sales as their fee for FBA products.

The cool thing is as well, if you do have a successful product selling, then you can launch a companion product to that, and you already have customers which you know will be interested. So it's entirely possible to build a full on brand using Amazon as your launching platform.

The drawback with Amazon FBA is that competition is fierce. It is currently one of the most popular business opportunities online, and as such, there are a lot of new sellers rushing in. The other potential hurdle is that since November 2016, the business became drastically more difficult overnight. What happened in November 2016 you ask? Well, this is when Amazon decided that incentivized reviews were no longer allowed on the site. The effect this had for FBA sellers was that the usual product launch strategy of giving away 50 or 100 products and getting an equal number of reviews in return was no longer valid.

Now review strategies vary from having family and friends leave reviews (risky and not a long term option) to running competitions on social media. Needless to say, it's a lot more time consuming, and costly, than it once was. However, there is still a lot of money to be made. Amazon keeps expanding year on year and the customer base is something that cannot be disputed. One thing I would urge you to look out for if deciding to go the Amazon FBA route, particularly if you are going to buy a course or training from someone. See if they have still had success after the change in review policy in 2016 - if they have, then they are someone who knows what they are doing.

Dropshipping

Here's an ecommerce business model that you may or may not have heard of. It's one that comes up often if you "making money online" - yet a lot of people don't truly understand how it works, or just explain it incorrectly.

Here is dropshipping in one sentence - With dropshipping, you essentially act as a middle man between supplier and customer.

In other words, you set up a store selling, say, lampshades. You never keep any lampshades in stock yourself, instead, when a customer makes an order - you purchase the item from a third party, the supplier, and then have it shipped directly to the customer.

So you have zero inventory and don't need to own a warehouse full of product. You don't need to handle the shipping and handling either because the supplier does that. This makes dropshipping a pretty easy business to get into because all you need is a product to sell, a market to sell it to and a website to sell it from.

This gives dropshipping an inherent advantage over the Amazon FBA model because you don't need to order a ton of stock in advance. Your overhead costs are also a lot lower because you really just need a laptop, a domain name, and web hosting - the latter two can be had for less than $100 a year. Which makes dropshipping attractive to many first time ecommerce entrepreneurs who may not have the necessary capital to pursue an Amazon FBA business for example.

What kind of products sell well via dropshipping, well here's a few that I found while searching online

- Bluetooth headphones
- Pet accessories (particular dog accessories)
- Stress balls
- Heart rate monitors (like heart rate watches)
- Art supplies
- Reusable shopping bags with designs on them (a lifestyle item rather than just a shopping bag)

How do people find your website? Mainly through paid advertising on search engines like Google and Bing. If your store ranks on the first page for a given search term then it's likely that you're going to receive a fair amount of traffic. However, that's petty tough to do for a brand new site, which is why paid traffic is so important for dropshipping stores. Obviously, the more competitive the category your store is in, the more you will be paying to acquire customers. This is something to bear in mind if you decide to go the dropshipping route.

Another area to consider is that unlike Amazon FBA, you don't get a say in the product design or labelling. Which leads us to the main problem with the dropshipping model. And this problem is one of the margins. Because there is little differentiation between your product and a competitor store for example - it's really a race to the bottom in terms of prices. Plus, as dropshipping becomes a more popular business model, it means niches get saturated quickly as the only way people can compete is on price. The lack of product differentiation or branding means it's almost impossible to build a brand by using a dropshipping model. Going back to margins, it is not uncommon to see a dropshipping business with $1 million in revenue only making $30K a year profit due to razor thin margins. Bare this in mind if you see someone advertising their success.

Another issue is a logistical one. As lots of dropshipping stores owners use products from different suppliers, it makes logistics like shipping difficult to track. Like being able to promise certain delivery times if you have to rely on various factories around the world. This means if something goes wrong like the supplier forgets to ship the product, then you are on the hook. Because the customer isn't aware that you are dropshipping goods, and expects that you are fulfilling the orders yourself.

Dropshipping has become an increasingly attractive business model in the past few years, and for good reason. It's probably the lowest barrier to entry ecommerce business, even lower than Kindle publishing. However, it is more of a short term cashflow business than something you can build into a viable long term asset for yourself, in my opinion at least.

Merch by Amazon

This is another ecommerce opportunity which utilizes the Amazon platform. Except for this time you aren't selling physical widgets like yoga mats or silicone chopping boards, you're selling clothing.

Still relatively unknown, Amazon opened up this print on demand program at the end of 2016, but at the time of writing (June 2018), it's now very accessible. Whereas you previously had to wait a long time to be accepted (my own application took 11 months), now it's possible to get accepted in a matter of days.

When you are first accepted into the program, you get to pick up to 10 different t-shirt designs. If just one of these sells within the first 180 days of your account being accepted, then your account stays open. The program operates on a tier system, so the more t-shirts you sell, the more designs you can upload.

The real beauty of all this is that because this is a print on demand service, you don't have to pay money upfront to get a batch of t-shirts made. You simply upload your designs onto pre-made templates, choose 5 colors and you're good to go. Similar to Amazon FBA, Amazon themselves handles the shipping process, but as they print the t-shirts, you don't have to send in a bunch of designs up front or anything like that.

This sounds relatively simple, but there is a lot of competition and many popular niches like pet lovers have been saturated pretty quickly. Because of this, I wouldn't get into Merch by Amazon expecting to make thousands per month right off the bat. However, it is entirely possible to add a few hundred per month to your bank account in a completely passive manner.

The key here is having cool designs (duh!) but also being able to get into low competition niches because otherwise you will be forced to compete on price and your profit margins will be near non-existent.

If you're not a graphic designer, then there are a few places where you can get inexpensive designs made like Fiverr or Upwork. Other pricier options include sites like 99designs where different designers can bid on work for you.

Although it is competitive, I still recommend the Merch by Amazon program as a solid way to make money because of the low startup costs and easy logistical nature of the business. You won't be set for life from it, but there is a good chance you can make a few hundred extra dollars each and every month.

Self Publishing Books on Amazon

Publishing a book you say? What a ridiculous concept. From the outside, it does sound fairly ridiculous, self publishing books on a variety of topics and expecting people to buy them. Well, as a matter of fact, they do. Millions of customers are searching Amazon.com every single day for books about everything from how to sew, losing weight with a certain kind of diet, and even yo-yo tricks.

I'm biased, but this is one of my favorite ways to make money online. It's got one of the lowest barriers to entry when compared to other ecommerce businesses. In fact, you can get started for as little as $500. You don't need any technical skills or expensive software to begin your self publishing business either.

In fact, one six figure publisher I know started with absolutely 0 and did everything himself. I wouldn't recommend doing this because it's a huge time suck.

But it is entirely possible if you're truly broke when starting out.

With this particular money making venture, you operate similarly to how you would with any Amazon based business. In that, you leverage Amazon's gigantic levels of traffic, and people already searching for books on certain topics. From there, you publish (note: not write) a book on that particular topic.

When I say you don't have to write books - I mean. There are many ghostwriting companies that can write a full book for you in as little as 10 days for as little as $150. Alternatively, you can hire freelancers on websites like Upwork to write your book for you. Then there's also the option of writing the book yourself - but for most people, the time involved is just too much.

You can publish either fiction or non-fiction books, personally, I think non-fiction has a lower barrier to entry. I've also learned that fiction has higher income potential at the top end, so it's really your call at the end of the day.

The trick comes in being able to position your book from a unique angle, which you'll be able to do with some customer research. By doing this, you can stand out from the crowd and elevate your book above the competition.

You don't need a sales or marketing background to do this either. Most of it comes from just reading customer reviews on Amazon books, seeing what people liked and didn't like - then tweaking them your own book to be better than the competition.

The great thing about Kindle publishing is that Amazon handles everything for you. Once your book is uploaded onto the Kindle platform, you don't have to do anything else. Making this a fantastic passive income opportunity.

This allows you to build a useful side income in just a few hours a week. There are even successful publishers earning $10,000+ a month while working less than 10 hours a week. Imagine being able to run your entire business from the beach?

Here's where Kindle publishing really shines though, you can use it to get more than one stream of income. You can use Amazon's print on demand platform Createspace to sell physical books. These physical books give you much higher royalties than Kindle ebooks (usually 3 to 7 times higher), so it's a great extra stream of income. There's also the potential for you books to get into brick and mortar stores like Barnes & Noble by using Createspace - how cool is that?

You can also upload your book onto Audible, which Amazon also owns - which then gives you a third stream of income from that same book. How many other products are there which allow you to get three streams of income!

So what kind of books are you publishing - well here are the top 5 niches for non-fiction self publishing books

1.Making money online

2.Weight loss

3.Self help

4.How-to guides

5.Cookbooks (although personally, I don't recommend you go into this niche)

These books all have very high customer demand, so if you can publish a unique book, for example, "how to make money online with a sewing blog", then anyone with a sewing blog will automatically be interested in what you have to say.

You can then take thing even further by using your books to promote complementary products like physical products in that niche.

The main drawback of self publishing is the capped income levels on the front end. Because you are selling low priced products, and there is a lot of competition in many keywords, it's hard to break through to the multiple 6 figures a year level by only publishing books. Of course, this can be achieved by setting up a backend to drive your customers to additional offers. However, in terms of the business you can go from zero to $100,000 a year the fastest - self publishing may well be it

With a backend, there's also a potential to then scale your business using your books as a way to promote affiliate products (although Amazon has rules determining how you can do this - so make sure you always comply with them). This backend is where you can really tap into Amazon's potential, plus you will learn essential online business skills like email marketing along the way.

Utilizing Self Publishing Books to Market Your Services

Here's something you don't hear a lot of people discussing. The advantages of using books in your marketing funnel.

Say you're a personal trainer who gets clients online. Or any online service provider for that matter. One of your biggest hurdles to overcome in this kind of business is getting traffic.

Well little did you know - Amazon is actually one of the world's largest search engines. And the great thing about Amazon customers is, they are already looking for things to buy. As opposed to merely searching for free information about a certain topic.

In fact, Amazon is the 10th largest site in the world by total traffic, and by far and away the largest E-Commerce website. So having a presence there is a great way to leverage traffic. Plus, it's far easier to rank a book high on Amazon, than it is to rank a blog post highly on Google.

Think about it from a positioning standpoint as well. How many other people in your niche have a book for sale? Not just a 2 page PDF available for download on their website either.

We're talking about an honest-to-goodness physical book which people can touch. This does wonders for your service business. It elevates you above your competition and allows you to charge more for your service. You will also have clients coming to you, rather than the other way around. Some food for thought at the very least.

Two online businesses I recommend you to avoid

Multi-Level Marketing (MLM)

MLM, also called network marketing is one of the more controversial ways of making money online. It is often sold as a chance to own your own business with zero overhead and zero employees to take care of. This sounds great in theory, however, it just isn't that simple. For that reason, the MLM model is similar to affiliate marketing, except there is one key difference between the two.

In affiliate marketing, you are referring people to a product - they buy the product and you get a commission.

In MLM, you are referring people to the company or system itself. You get a commission when they sign up.

Many MLM companies charge a fee to join. These fees are can be small like $100 for a few items of inventory, or a large annual subscription to have the right to sell the products. Most have their own products that they sell, which as a member of the company, you can also sell as an affiliate. However, where a lot of these companies come under fire is that the products themselves are of a low quality, so the demand for them is inherently low. Therefore to make any money as part of an MLM company, you have to promote the company itself. As you've already spent money on inventory, you then need to do this as a way to make your money back.

To promote the company you must recruit new members to the program, for doing so, you often get a percentage of their commissions as well. However, as these new members also need to make money, they must also recruit new members. If that all sounds ridiculous, then the diagram below gives a visual representation of how it all works. You'll now also realize why MLMs are synonymous with the term "pyramid scheme" because that's exactly how it works. The few at the top make all the money whereas those at the bottom make next to nothing (and often lose money for joining)

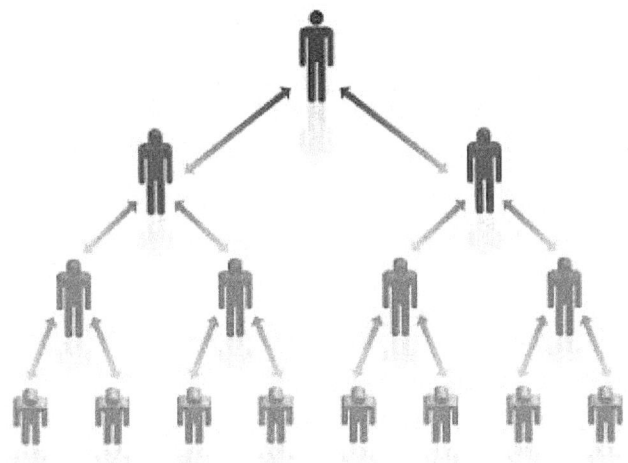

Because of this, the vast majority of people involved in MLM do not make any money. Simply because there aren't enough people in their spheres of influence to recruit.

One final word on MLMs and this is important. Because many people who join MLMs have no business experiences and no way to recruit customers - they often target their friends first. By target I mean, you know those posts you see on Facebook titled "GOT AN AMAZING OPPORTUNITY FOR YOU - pm me for details". This is especially prevalent among middle aged women, a demographic which a lot of MLMs target. Here is one such example (names removed)

Grady M. Polcyn
Have you ever had a prospect say, "This is Business is Amazing...but I don't have any money " ???

PROBLEM SOLVED
Interesting SOURCE of $$$ for prospects needing Cash to Start Vemma from Christopher Jackson Vemma Team Familia:

Just a tip to get ppl in the company quicker if money is an issue. This website called cashnetusa.com lets ppl with bank accts borrow up to 1000 dollars and deposit in banking acct in 2 business days when you receive the money you can set up a payment plan for no extra charge. I use this all the time. My friend just took out a loan for 500 and has to pay back 620 and he set up a payment plan for 100 dollars every 2 weeks with no extra charge!!!!! Hmu for more info. #rackem
www.cashnetusa.com

Online Loans & Online Payday Loans | CashNetUSA.com
www.cashnetusa.com
Apply for online personal loans quickly & get cash the next business day! Choose from payday, installment, or line of credit loans.

 Like · Comment · Follow Post · Share

👍 21 people like this.

💬 View 12 more comments

Kelly Diebel will they accept those who have bad or no credit?
2 hours ago · Like

So not only is being part of an MLM often bad for your wallet, it's often bad for your friendships as well.

If it sounds like I'm being overly negative towards MLMs, then that's fair. However, my argument is supported by facts. Depending on the company, the percentage of people who lose money in MLM ranges from 95 to 99%. I've even seen some figures as high as

99.6%, and believe me if someone on your Facebook feed comes asking if you want to join - it's unlikely that either you or they will be part of the 99.6%.

Let's do a specific example, here is one company Arbonne. The company sells beauty products, which is a popular niche for MLM companies.

As an Arbonne member, you get 35% commission of sales of the products themselves, and then 15% commission on sales made by anyone you recruit to the program. The following screenshot was taken from the official Arbonne website, as all MLMs are required to disclose member's earnings.

Average Annual Earnings of Active Arbonne Independent Consultants for 2017

	Average Annual Earnings	Top 50 Average	Bottom 50 Average	Average % of Active Arbonne Independent Consultants	Average Months to Promote
National Vice Presidents	$254,101	$582,409	$90,809	1%	56
Regional Vice Presidents	$68,110	$132,418	$23,951	2%	36
Area Managers	$17,129	$54,620	$2,702	7%	21
District Managers	$3,450	$20,413	$86	28%	7
Independent Consultants	$788	$8,252	$17	62%	n/a

So 97% of Arbonne members make less than $17,000 a year and a whopping 90% of them make $3,450 or less per year in revenue. Note, these figures are <u>revenue</u>, so this does not include any expenses like buying inventory or any advertising costs for example. I wouldn't hesitate to say that those in the bottom 90% are likely losing money in their "business".

This right here is the number one reason why I suggest you <u>do not</u> join any MLM schemes.

It's also the reason that many MLMs come under fire from regulatory bodies, here is just a short list of MLMs which have been shut down over the past few years

- Digital Altitude
- Bitconnect
- DavorCoin
- Vacation Club
- WakeUpNow
- ForexEntourage

And here are some companies still in business which have the hallmarks of MLM business.

- Herbalife
- Lipsense
- NuSkin
- Rodan & Fields
- Vemma
- Primerica

Anyway, I hope you've enjoyed this chapter - because I consider it one of the most important in the book. Unfortunately, when getting started online, many people fall for the MLM model and end up losing money in the process. Now you've seen the truths behind this predatory model, we'll move onto the some more positive business models.

Update: As of June 10th 2018, it appears My Online Business Education (MOBE, also known as MTTB) has been shut down by the FTC. This was another prominent multi-level marketing company

Day trading cryptocurrency/forex

Day trading cryptocurrency/forex

I see this being promoted as an online business opportunity all over social media. It started with forex (foreign currency) but the number of offers seems to have multiplied seen the middle of 2017 when Bitcoin and other cryptocurrencies really started taking off.

Online financial trading in any form is inherently risky. You are liable to lose a lot of money if you don't know what you are doing. With cryptocurrency, this is magnified because of the sheer volatility of the market. It's not uncommon for a coin to drop in value by 50% in a single day.

Trading is a risky profession, depending on which source you use, between 90 and 92% of traders wind up losing money. This is because there are so many factors that go into becoming a successful trader. It's not just technical analysis either, there is a myriad of emotional and psychological factors at play as well. Because remember, you re staring at screens watching your money fluctuate on a minute by minute basis - that reeks havoc on the brains of even the calmest people.

In fact, here's a quote from successful day trader and author James Altucher

"I was a day trader for many years, and it almost killed me."

You must have herculean self discipline in order to be successful in trading, especially with cryptocurrency. It's all well and good when the market is going up like we saw at the end of 2017. But once the market starts trending sideways or downwards, that's what separates the men from the boys (or the women from the girls - I don't discriminate).

Remember, you can't predict the future in financial markets. You may think you can, but you can't. Trading is filled with uncertainty and unforeseen events. For an lot of traders, especially less sophisticated ones, online trading is no more than a form of gambling. Except instead of sports teams or horses, they are betting on cryptocurrencies or the value of the Japanese Yen.

The other drawback to financial trading as an entry level way to make money online is a financial one. You will need a significant amount of capital to get started. You may see a few blogs and YouTube videos telling you about rags to riches stories where the owner turned an initial investment of $100 into $1,000,000 by trading stocks/forex/cryptocurrency - but these stories are likely to be embellished at the very least or just completely untrue altogether.

Most full time traders started with a capital amount of 5 figures, so $10,000 or more. You need this amount to cover the commission fees you have to pay every time you execute a trade, along with any potential losses you may make along the way. Another thing to consider is that most trading platforms usually have a minimum fee involved, which can be as high as $19 per trade. So if you're only planning on starting at $200, 10% is taken away each time you make a trade. This is huge when we are talking about low profit margins, to begin with, because contrary to what some may tell you, making even 5% profit on a trade is considered a good win. You also won't come out on the winning side on every trade, in fact, a win/loss ratio of 55/45 is what most professional traders are content with. That means if you have a streak of losing trades, which can, and most probably will happen - you need enough of a bankroll to cover this. All of this is just not possible if you only have a few hundred dollars to start with.

One final note on this, I'm not saying that you shouldn't invest in stocks, or cryptocurrencies at all. That's a perfectly valid way of managing and growing your money. But investing and actively trading are two very different sides of the coin, and the latter is what I discourage if you are just starting out and are looking for a way to grow your online income.

The most important skill to learn if you want to be successful in business in 2018 and beyond

This is a question I get a lot. Is there one particular skill you should learn if you want to be successful online in 2018? There is an answer to this, and that answer is as follows.

If you are going to learn one skill, it should be how to sell

I can hear you through the screen right now groaning inside. Sales?! Selling conjures up a negative reaction from a lot of people. They get reminded of a sleazy used car salesman who lies and tricks you into buying a crappy car. Others may think sales involves "forcing" people to buy your product through a series of tactics, but that couldn't be further from the truth.

Well, that's not the kind of sales I'm talking about. I'm talking about ethical persuasion here. The art and science of demonstrating that you have a product or service that is valuable to someone and that you should be fairly compensated in return for exchanging this to them. This makes the entire transaction a win-win as opposed to the used car salesman example which is a zero-sum game (he wins, you lose).

Selling is vital when starting out in business because your ability to acquire customers will determine your initial success. Sure, once you have built a solid foundation of business there are other skills which will be useful as well. But when going from zero to 7 figures, your sole goal should be to acquire as many customers as possible.

This applies just as much to a physical products business as it does to a service based business. The only difference is the "what" you are selling. The mechanics are the same, demonstrating to a potential customer that you have something which will enrich their lives in one way or another.

A big misconception with sales is that it is a natural ability, one that people are innately born with. They often associate it with charismatic, extroverted people and think they because they are shy, introverts that selling is something they simply can't do. Well, that is complete rubbish because anyone can learn how to sell.

The first thing to understand is that not all selling has to be done face-to-face or on the phone. In fact, when talking about online business, the vast majority of your sales will be done without speaking to a prospect or having any sort of 1 to 1 interaction with them.

When selling online, your main job is uncovering people's problems, and solving them. This can be in the form of a physical product, a digital product or a service you are offering. But all three of these do the same job, they solve a problem or a set of problems for the buyer.

If you can tap into people's real problems, which may be different from the ones that appear on the surface, you don't need to speak to them face to face, if you can demonstrate that you have the solution. You can do this through words, through video or through audio - but as long as you can show you understand the problem, you are good.

In the free bonus book *How to Develop an Unbreakable Mindset*, I go more in-depth about how learning sales can also teach you valuable life lessons which will help further your online business career.

Final thoughts

I hope you've enjoyed reading this book and that you got a lot of value out of the ideas I have discussed inside it. I've had a lot of struggles and setbacks in my own online marketing journey, and I hope you can learn from some of the mistakes that I made.

A big part of writing this book was not only to dispel some of the myths about making money online (that it's impossible/expensive/too late to get into), but to also give back in a way, because without certain figures on the internet, I myself would have probably never had been able to make the money I have or live the lifestyle I am currently living.

Making money online is truly a fantastic way of life. Waking up knowing that you have money coming in every day. Being able to work from anywhere, whether that's your home office, in a hammock or on the beach (although the screen glare is a real issue which not enough online marketers are talking about).

It liberates you from traffic filled commutes, annoying co-workers, bosses who have nothing but dislike for you (and vice versa).

It gives you the time to spend with family, friends and loved ones.

Time to dedicate to your interests, whether that be scuba diving in Indonesia, horseback riding across Mongolia, skydiving in New Zealand. Or even something as simple as waking up in the morning, and enjoying a cup of freshly brewed coffee on the porch with your spouse, safe in the knowledge you don't have to rush off to work in 10 minutes.

So what's the next step? Because I don't want you to put this book down, say "that was a nice read" and then do nothing. The good news is, I have a another book for you.

You see, the mechanics of online marketing are just part of the equation, which is why I wrote the bonus book *How to Develop an Unbreakable Mindset* which is available for free using the link below.

In this short guide I go through the various hurdles and mental challenges you need to overcome in order to be successful online.

This also includes reversing some of the negative beliefs that you have probably (I know I did) picked up along the way. You have acquired these beliefs through no fault of your own, but as a result of our education systems and the beliefs of society at large - which are slowly instilled into us during our formative years.

You can get your free copy by going to

http://el-gorr.com/unbreakable

Just some final words, a huge thank you again from me. Every time someone downloads this book I consider it a personal milestone, and I hope you enjoyed reading it.

Thanks,

Oliver